on(3) time

on(3) time

maija mist

New York

on(3) time
copyright ©2022 maija mist. All Rights Reserved.

thanks to terra at recenter press, erica at spectra poets,
ashley & the team at metatron press, & perennial press.

& thanks to my FaMily for helping me to Sea ;
for allowing site .
to rāj & our baba hanuman
4 evrever

ho'oponopono
amor amor
asé asé

cover art: Tola Cohia Brennan

ARTEIDOLIA PRESS
New York

www.arteidolia.com/arteidolia-press

First Edition
Library of Congress Control Number: 2022919019
ISBN: 978-1-7369983-6-6

"For in my blindness the vision
did evoke from my stricken mind
a fantastic reflex of itself, an echo,
a symbol, a myth, a crazy dream,
contemptibly crude and falsifying,
yet, as I believe,
not wholly without significance."

Olaf Stapledon, Starmaker

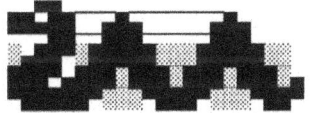

"There is no truth but a coincidence
of all truths."

Rudolf Steiner

```
c    o   n   t        en ts         ///
       contents  \\  s  \          co
n          tnts               \\\
con              t      en          ts
     cont     e                \  ||||
                   n   t  s         \c
\o\\n\\|t\/e/nts/       ✺ ✺ ✺
```

& again ::: 1
reconciliation /// happenstance may make its plan ::: 2
re: pixels ::: 3
convalescenc ::: 4
subliminatin ::: 5
write it ::: 6
foxglove ::: 7
crossbreeze &nd   th roof @nite ::: 8
shower thouht ::: 9
the thing is ::: 10
th stckr emporium ::: 12
satellite s gone ::: 13
grimes' garden ::: 14
dntwtchtv ::: 15
lo fi hip hop beets ::: 16
selenite ::: 17
tender roots ::: 18
tru luv will find u in th end ::: 19
pylon ::: 20
it lasts a while &nd tht is   wnderfull ::: 21
apotheosis s ::: 22
babe* ::: 23
evergreen nevermine ::: 24
tub ::: 25

reckless ::: 26
lintel ::: 27
btwn astral &etheric ::: 28
obser vationl   d rawin g ::: 29
endurance is key ::: 30
flatbush ::: 32
halcyon ::: 33
p a c i f i c ::: 34
gnomon ::: 35
o r c h i d ::: 36
eudalypt us ::: 37
dawn ::: 38
if yu   want   it ::: 39
decided to go to th bar ::: 40
local anesthesia ::: 41
everything bagel pls ::: 42
arcadia ::: 43
maybe it s not ::: 44
los angeles ::: 45
king tai ::: 46
ff ::: 47
linetime ::: 48
do yu remember rock&rollradio ::: 49
s ::: 50
thoughts 4 thots ::: 51
&nd   if so ::: 52
3am btwn ::: 53
mauna ::: 54
c o g n itiv   dissona nc ::: 55
yes &nd ::: 56
cntrl arm ::: 57
paregoric vile or ::: 58
trinket casing ::: 59

1-2 step ::: 60
neptune ::: 61
thchosn1 ::: 62
get me where ::: 63
find me everywhere so i know it s real ::: 64
candiiland ::: 65
the drums the drums ::: 66
111 ::: 67
amber brew ::: 68
hearing different things ::: 69
"" i wasn t on it - yu were in it "" ::: 70
sing while sleeping ::: 71
twrds creation of no thing ::: 72
aho ::: 73
phosphorescence ::: 74
soulfly ::: 75
individualize myth ::: 76
durian ::: 77
cloroform ::: 78
sweetness ::: 79
yr past is a ghost ::: 80
something else ::: 81

& again

space is small   & recurring
we re   meant to circle in on each othr

rising while   sinking &   the time is rite

uncomfortabl @ the party   he lafd   a bit
describing the folk bar

bc we all take what we want
anyways   jus   take it all &nd
take it all till the bits make th cornrs curl

winter creation like   slo gray leaves

&   i   m   listnng to othr ppl agin
figuring out how much   is my own

how to drop the vowel   lick the tip

swrl it round   &   hang on the dispensr
lean on th levr   rub it in2 my chest

aftr the sprl stops

                               faster still getting still move
                               the dial slower faster left of
                               the dial once in a lifetime

reconciliation /// happenstance may make its plan //

                th quiet mind knows no bounds
                                 unbound

                  $\geq$ tried & tru $\leq$
            this time around we found
            · ° ° • reunited states •° ° ·

th speakr yu bought me in midtown
up &down a few escalators
                    said yu need this
                    & i did

    a timeline for dissolution & vows
    held fervently2 what yu knw i could be
    now that i am realizd   break to let it happen

+++ smashed mirror undr th gradient of the show +++

              everyone wants a piece
              everyone   wants
              veneer & vehemence
              fervor   &   freedom
              just th essence of what may be &
              a dream of holdng somethng that
              is not their own

floating   free
smell of sage   in th water
sound of self   thru th mirror

re: pixels

                wht your seeng now is just

                              catching up

       don t worry bb

thru the eyes of th avatar   nothing is unreal

              surrendrng is no   passive act

    & nothng from outside   gives a feelng

                confrmatn thru   flashng lites

    don t pontificate

    forget th details

                be brief

convalescenc

when yu make it thru th past all you can do is   l is t it out
futur timelines that align in th rite places &nd we re back at it
g. says th plots b e come pivotl th more people involvd
yu know this

   every 3rd day there has been a
        fractured   lite shining i n

              we calculate th progression along th cave wall
                                          &nd add it to th list

caught up in   future   vision &nd
i need t stop befor i get carried away

yu wuld think so much   destruction
wuld take th roles   along   with it

                 i allways hoped it wuod

put thm in a timeline where ownrshp
was irrelevant &nd
fire was abundant

                   we ll   see how it pans out

                         o cast iron skillet
                         o braids
                         o lime puree
                         o collection
                         o wool socks

subliminatin

out of th clouds int th mist
like th d r o nes   at it   again &nd
th stomach   d r o p   &nd th
marks of l i t e in t h   periph e ry

e v e r y one   looks   li k e   u   now
i thnk it goes away &nd it s back again
s t e a d y   r e m i n d e r i m not here
i made some promises   but   you re
dzzlng hotels &nd low back   blck shrts
i s a y   things &nd don t   realiz   they
make it   worse off
th connect ion   is inescapabl b u t i
floundr   when it s not writtn

yu were fine befre yu ll b fine again
th glimps is enugh   to drag yu out
how yu think   there s somethng bettr
&nd kno   there s   s omethng worse

l i f t off &nd watch th t i d e s r ise
take me   back t th willow &nd
let me feel   f i n g r s   in my h a i r

it s always a little later that it shws up
somewhere else

i m   h e r e to make   it safer but i
covr   th markngs   w   s m o k e
i watch it all   fast forwr d   &nd
look t o w a r d s th inevitable rewind

think   th   th ought s   to decide
reel in the   need for too much els
filling up w a t e r to fill up w a t e r

ready to wtch th movie start to finish

write it

       sometimes   in a day
       plastic   flowers   on th sidewlk
       yr   kind   of   trash or   mine

                 in t e rmi t t e n t   come down
                 when you   least expect it   or
                 u n c ov r   th   need

figurng out th spce btwnth land

    th wovn layrs of each for now

               listening   to yr own   voice is
               d ist nct   m e d icine

               r e m ember   to   fo rg et

foxglove

in about a mnth we can be out in th open without a care
th state has   oth r thngs   to wrry about when th   weather turns

th lite helps   no s pot lite s
when b r i t e t n e s s   is   a   c o n s tnt

intrnl growth hs stuntd r maxd out r both
so seasons aren t much more thn moods

core gurglngs   o r   s l o   b u r n s

n   excuse to get caught up n th   fantasy
r delusion or th way it already has bn

eithr way ,
we do what we can to make it seem like keepng post s   more
thn jst going deep in2 what no one else can touch

th firewrks may b celebratory   aftr all
w e   n e e d   it
if anythng s tru   ,   it s   that
i   imagine when i set thm off   ,
th world ll be rid of firewrks fr g o o d

                        it s   wh a t   we ve   b e e n

               w a i t n g   f o r

crossbreeze &nd   th roof @nite

                    gettng clear & cleaning it up

                        past the point now

                                i am sure of what i am till
                                i am sure of something else

          bits enter in and return when they are needed most

paraphrasing does not belong to anyone

                knowing when to stop or
                documenting th progress

                      forceful movements and bodies like waves
                          moving up against the barricade

the tragedy of certainty
the clarity of the void

shower thouht

                i take what   p eople give me
                i write it down and save it fr ltr

      entir lifetims c ould be spent mining this lifetim

      i could focus on any 1 thng nd that would b enugh

befor the storm cam th renaissance & it is analog just like us
play it back for me   th eruption never gets old

                                    i keep buying 2ndhnd candls
                      1 s a purpl flwr the leaves mlts inwrd

                                            again

                            we ve been doing this all along

the thing is

steps twrds   u
                    the vision each time   getting slo
                       moving twrds the one ✻   in whtevr form

entrancd   & stepping solidly
lift up watch the tides rise
beeneath the ///   screen

frames come back for reuse   left & regained
                                         place by place

are you loosing yr sense of smell they ask   no no
can you breath under there   moist & swallw

((((hidden conception of any nuance))))

                                        drty cmp
                                        little sine
                                        alone again

                                        dusty mist

               >>> clarity of mvmnt
               g train twrds >>> or

✪ went to look at a lot
✪ went to the grocery store
✪ went to meet you to with a bag of laundry
✪more weed or

                                   i am clearing the forest
                                   i am weeding between weeds
                                   i am sure of not one thing
                                   i am sure of it

th stckr emporium

                                  penciled an explosion into my daily planner
                                       it came when it wanted to anyways

light heats up the inside
s   get it while its good

you can fall in love with anyone
again for the people in the back

compared our handwritng but i don t think about you now
writing is a lie   this is my magnum opus
fame and fortune   expert timing
flip a round like a slug that s lost it s way   aligning
&nd slurping off

thick straps a round the ankles
always   rollng the ankls

sav me from myself   now i m
plane hopping and growing fangs   ta ta

how is it that you never really learned how to draw a wave?

satellite s gone

jupiter s fog and th love songs again
walking down th street where we talked th firs time
i arrived &nd we keep arrivng

    some mansions i never thought i would live in the vicinity of

               he says you need to say what u want
               as we ride electri c   scooters   high
               n e x t   to   av o c a d o   tr e e s

    back in new york on the roof every night
    piecing togethr   th songs
    the stairs   th   l a d d r s
    t h   b r o k n   pl a t e s
    getting high to write   or

    snappin g   my   jaw   back into place
    pressing   till   i feel   h uman   ag n

or back to yur couch in th small room w no windows
where i tried vr for the frst time

            labels on containers &nd a s w i f t   p a s s n g

grimes' garden

when u fight to stay in this realitea ... ∞ ✿
               ✶ there s a frame in the garden
               ✶ there s   f u z z   in the   chain‰link

so happii 2 find you here
i don t   need   the   p h y s icality
justsum books on the chair & a green porch

change what ((word)) when
what sticks   --- ---
what stick s --- ---

               ✺ find the void in expert time
               ✺ recycl the all ✂ ☺ ☯

dntwtchtv

    >>>   a friend recommended a show today
a breedng ground for something they found in themselvs
   &␣nd   recogniz blossomng need for in a version of me

th way it may make you more whole
in th   same way
in interfring wys

i hav an app for my breathcount
an app to expand th confines of being
of bodyhood
of americn football suburbs

th word smells writtn n differnt ways here &nd
((there there))
memries mostly worlds of my own creation
no groundng in words or events
just th way yr eyes grazed mine

sry to say

th   g r o u n d w o r k
appearng disappeerng reappearng
always wth a   different motivatng force
left for me to   deconstruct
&nd   reconstruct

a licking of th lips , i suppose

lo fi hip hop beets

        the sky is a funny shade   of orange blue
        & i m thinking   of   migration as usual
        logos i   hav seen   time and t me again
        faded   versions or   on fresh plastc glass

        so few structurs   facilitate wellbeing
        so i   made m own   a trepidation
        for some   a heavenly   lull for othrs
        heds in laps   a petting of hair
        artificial baseball fields i think i liked onc
        the   girls   team   was   bussed   away
        a slo   shiftng   that   stops   wen
        yu   forget   it s   happning

    nobody asked for this but i m   doing it anyways
    to embrace a character of choice is quite an achievement

selenite

how re you selfmedicatng　　　　these days
is your　grlfrnd　　still　on your case　about it

thoug hts about　people yu ve　loved
talks about the　　formation of things

in btw　th　　s ongs　　　　btwn　th　li me li te
there　　s a glimpse of what came before　　　&
what comes again

　　　　　　　　　　　　　back like th last time

tender roots

        BRAID &   drive together
                      no nothing

    peak & pull 000 same direction extended loop
    hit of the hologram   liteleak   transparency

3vrsns aligning to remind me what it was like to fall asleep   &
wake up in different homes   other homes   my own & pit stops
along the way with crisp sheets & tight bodies   got somewhere
got it good   keep reminding me   keep finding the invitation
                       at a different post office   in a new town

remembered the myth & thought it better to sleep & breath

      difference thru repeated actions
      root the knowing
honeysuckle   &   daffodil
      known solidification
      in expansion

      e n chanted
      release any explanation
      or make it juicy comedy

tru luv will find u in th end

is this what it look s like
fingers softly hangglidng off th   moon

an overpass at nite

beam to centr

                                                                         i want
                                                                        to feel
                                                                      whatevr
                                                                     you thnk
                                                                       i shuld

                           an overpass at nigh t

                                beam 2 center

saved / safe in the spirit stash
i said i nvr have but i alwys hav

writing is the devil & i have been caught for decades

beats let it up & out

pylon

caroline is picking flowers &nd tying them into knots
i put them around her head &nd we spin around till we fall

she s a mom in another stry   she says she has learnd so much

if it   allows for   reflection
            it   is   enough

                                    where yu want   to be is
                                    unfoldng in everyone els
                                    f o r g e &nd   let it fall

i set thm off &nd we watch a str shw rflctd in th sky
mist i n t e r m i n g l e s   &nd th spots convulse
all   there   is   to   do   now   is   lie   down

it lasts a while &nd tht is   wnderfull

rmembrng th last time&nd fast frwrdng
j   u   s   t   a   b   i   t

choices leave   n o   middle ground

going out t buy toothpste &nd tampons

creation lifestyle   no tools r extricatin

slip n slides ,   grocery stores ,   water parks ,   air shows ,
exploshins   ,   root vegetables

inherent knowing
                              amidst chaos

what do yu think of my new bathngsuit

c o l ored   p a p e r   &nd   pencils

markings t   indicate a life fully live d

repairng th baseboards   as needed

apotheosis s

                      don t forget th space b/w
                      body as pendulum
                      braid into the vessel

in my dream of y ur dream we are   confident in our ability
truth is recognized thru feeling
                            &nd a crooked spine realigns

                    hoovering mid air as a leaf fall s   to the ground
                    past the aloe plant   to the dirt floor

                    superseding th soundtrck that will be placed to it

                    glidng across th page as th pain leaves   th body

                    a state we will one day learn to make permanent

babe*

continued in weary style stepping outside
lightr in hand   the one they look for 2touch back down

        funeral party ::: this time it is easy
        nothing much to say && can you live with that
        rest locates meaning ,,, signified storyline

COFFEE
be the evidence
out in the country
somewhere you never wanted
& found

                harm lacks discernment
                push me past the point
                till i step outside myself

        release seduction by   overstimulation
        land home   evidence embodied

    some can see it all
    + + +
    + + +
    + + +

evergreen nevermine

built shelves   simultan eously
fr someone else after we ve   moved away

lookng out   on th same   streets
someday we ll go back   &nd
realize everything that   happend at once

dust t dust lkng nto th neighbrs   windws

in our tv sho i m starng down yur throgt
tellng yu how big   yr   tonsils look
tryng to   touc h thm with my tongue
while yur   friend   &nd mine   rubs out
th knots in my legs

smile whn th word comes back

                    what color ar ur sweatpnts

                    is ur girlfrnd runnng in place towrds th window

                    tied hands, backbones, and sequential motives

tub

th   b o y s
l i s t e n n g   to
something we ve
l i s t e n d   to
before on th roof
at a   s k i resort

                when yu wake from th dream you re still dreamng
                                                          of course

                a l i g n &nd r i s e   but th tides change &nd
                last nite i saw yr face in th r e f l e c t i o n
                t houht   maybe we could try

th lites change inside &nd out
p l s   do it just for me

reckless

last nite i watchd a   s t a r s h ow   in   th   slivr
b tween the shade nd th wall
i   c o n t r o l l e d   the st ar s   b u t   n o t   th   cloud s

there s a constnt airplane buzz tht gets loudr
at th utterance of certain p h rases

i imagine you into   acceptance of m y s l f
here we go a g a i n   reckless abandn
on a champagne supernova i n t h e s k y

                         love you in th   future vrsn futur
                         v i s i o n   i s   2 0 2 0

sing to me   she says
a hum &nd a dive off stage like
i t   used to b   nothing

lintel

g. says always curl arnd to b sure
when you get to th cave it s bettr to have seen it from th back
                                            beforehand

                                        a f e w days in
                                        &d it cn   start
                                        to seem   like
                                        yu w e r e nvr
                                        o u t t h e r e
                                        to begin with

but then yu need fire so th world seems more n line wth
wht you thouht it was

that &nd th more physical necessity of t

                        – 2 watr bottls

                        – liftd infinity sine

                        – c l o t h

                        – transparen c y

                        – som olives

btwn astral &etheric

nvrmind

obser vationl   d rawin g

repetition drawng lines btwn
p l a c e s   we   have been

frkwrks go off in th distance

a substitute for ears popping
or   anything else really

trips   n v r   as   containd
a s   they   o u g h t   to be

opening &nd clsng windows
f o r e v e r i n   a   d a y

endurance is key

th men of this wrld will have yu believe they contain guilt ()
what we hav bn shown but tend to forgt is that guilt is a
carefully constructd mechanism () a microprocessr emittng
nightshade that appeals t a general audienc () a way to flip it
on its side &nd show yu yr reflectun as a lesser of 2 evils ()
now there are orchids bloomng thru th cracks onc a yr &
we ar left to sit alone in front of ar tv that is turnd off
&nd wndr ()   i have alwys cringed at th violence () the incst
() the objcts floatng in and out of my periphery   () searching
regardless fr th stuff i believed i would find aftr all   ()
                                                    but all i did ws endure

i watchd th men around me emit terrifyng noises at a crsh
on th screen &nd fell into myself wunderng why i could not
produce such a pwrfl noise   () wht wld become of me
                                                                       if i failed

            falling into a figure8 and drifting away on cnyn rvr rpds
            round and round agn   i am called many things
            by many ppul   i learnd to paint my face to
            cntrl the noise   then calculatd the time spnt &nd
            fell into a sorrw of a half century   rising as a ghost
            an anonymous author whose preservation i fought for
            as a senile librarian in 1931

      we spend so much reflctng on time spent undr th thumb
      we forgt we forged lives after th sky broke   &nd
      allowd the light to come rushing in   formng
      frctals at every surface   repeating the process
      allowing awe to be the only f ling

i transfrmd myself into a pastel object causing polarized emotions
for specific purpos
not every life is the one   i tell myself

                         sitting on a bench   in central park
                         things here exist regardless of time
                         i have s u b m i t t e d   to the city
                         i will be here   after th fall
                       &nd before th grt war

sometimes i remember to be somewhere when i am supposd 2b
of course it doesn t always work out   &nd then i wondr more

flatbush

                jus tryng t get yu back in th rotatin

time reverses int wht has been   &nd
i m only seeing it all   from th   outside
but yu know i m tryng to work yu int my dreams

      let me kno if   that s okay

if i had to fill you in   on th
meniality of it all   i could
bu t i m   mor   interested
in putting my   head on
yr   shouldr

                            i don t nee d a lot
                            i need a lot of nothng

end th beautiful   statements   with a   reminder   that
it all came from yu   & has made a   life of its own

halcyon

dip into a　small　f e a s t
lush reds　　　candles up
& nd　　　　d　o　w　　n
d i s s　o l v n g　　f o o d
some t ea　　　afterwrds

　　　　　　　then a school of fish &nd m not so thirsty
　　　　　　　the tea was good　　　freshwater better
　　　　　　　b ubbles　make e v e r y　form　　smile

　　　　　✪ orange crush
　　　　　✪ sparks
　　　　　✪ surrender

pacific

        adaption thru   acknwldgmnt
        noise machines   or ear plgs
        d r w n i n g   o u t
        s o m e   l o o p   w/in me

        i m   not that which i cling to

        i said i wld go bck lst nite
        asif back   was th place i strtd
        &th   place to which   i
        m u s t   r e t u r n

        set   a n y thing   in motion
        h e r e   i   w i l l   be

gnomon

i m the one when the lites shut off ✦

                        it s n o t   t o o   m u c h
                        gettng   closer   to   th point
                        left th   record   spinnin g
                        &nd spun out th   computr spkrs
                        going   bck   int old trianglr states

looking for something i left curbside &nd forgot to pick up leaving th bar before i got on th bus   raining ✦✦✦✦✦✦✦ w a l k i n g c i r c u l a r l y smoking   cigarettes   under   the   cornr   store awning   aftr   it   had   closd   ✦✦✦✦✦✦✦

     one moment is enough to draw   many moments outside   of it

orch id

got som firewrks attachd to eithr side of me , if there comes
a time i need them   a   brthda y   p a r t y   o r   a n
assault   one   or th   othr   ,,   really   ha p p y
b i r thda y ,   ba b y,   it's a party,   it s   y r
                                                      birthday prty

o n e   o r   t h e   o t h e r   ,   i   repeat to myself
                                                 a f e w   t i mes
either / or   l ol

a nyway s ,   s. cut his hair off

or   died it deep purple with a beet
or   did some many things w/out me

the problm wth   givng into th   role

eucalypt us

                                        y ou ve   seen it befor
                                        top of   th mountain
                                        wth a brimmd hat &nd
                                        a backpck

                beckonng to th overlook where we watchd
                        the f i res   engulf the m ansions

                  your mom s firepit on new years eve
                  with my sunglasses   bt i wasn t there

chris said smetmes i just stay in n watch th suns collide

                                      wrote it for me to write it for me

waitng for th future life but eye m so happy in th downfall
what can happen bt one extreme   or the nxt

dawn

        th same song on repeat on my laptp
        until i   move   to   shut it down

        l y i n g   w   u   in b e d
        sheddng   layers   thru
        sweat   &nd   hard work

        yrs ago   when we met again
        writing ,   i want to believe
        on a chlkboard in   th   apt
        &nd   l e a v i n g   i t t h e r e
        for   quite some time

        running btwn my hous &nd claires

        takng picturs of ourselvs in mirrors
        home   amongst the t r i n k e t s
        being   a trinket for someone else

if yu want it

                    totality &nd movement
                    & n d the law of one
                    b l i ss ful   sur ren d er
                    audible befr it is visible

in an old victorian house that   i think belongs to the parents of someone i am dating () i go up the stairs &nd there is a shallow tub of liquid that you apply t body parts it tells you if energy is flowing based on the color that comes up when it is applied   () i dip one arm in && it is teal one arm is rose ()most of my chest && torso are rose and so are arms & legs save 1   muddy thigh my boyfriend comes in as i am trying to document the results () looking in a mirror says we should photograph it   we are late to something but everyone seems to think this is more importnt

collect evidence &nd continue
moving up the vibrational scale
broadcast what you   want
t u n e   to th   c h a n n e l
live in the vibration of   wonder

every time i am there someone feels like you as if to signify
i am in the right place &&
                                        you are always around

lite in the closet jus went off but there is no lite in the clost

decided to go to th bar

got a tecate &nd sat down in th corner seat
everyone was v a g u e l y   familiar
the   bartender   came   o ver   b/c
i lookd confusd &nd couldnt find my drink
i realized th tecate was there   &nd
i just couldn t see it from   certain angles

walking s o m e w h e re   w 2   w o m e n
@ a certain point i decidd i wanted to draw
nd askd th yngr womn to snd me a sktchbk
but she was like, um i can jus materialize it
&nd materialized it

i   started   d r a w in g
i   tried   to   explain lucid dreaming
2the womn running th hypnthrpy wrkshp
i asked for a radiator hospital   song to play
&nd then changed my mind
m a d e   n e w   d i rt p a th s

local anesthesia

        watch it go &nd   let it
        before nd after   once again

          a menial text or a
          milestone   visit

      dental care for the masses
         a crack in the rug

    planning a visit to plan a visit

  i m always th one to burn th house down

everything bagel pls

i love you more she said as if love was quantifiable
as if evry   benevolnt action led to the   next
blue light glasses   & a buzzing of crickets
a description is best met by other   descriptors
& taken down a   rabbit   hole of   fresh
scallion   cream cheese   & its counterparts

u lured me so well that time   as if quantm leapng
to a previous dilemma   & solving it before it ever
                    lured me here in the first place

                repetitive motions can make anything into something else

i try to find the words but alas
& as always i am trapped
              in a mess of all the makings
              with the makings

arcadia

        when the sounds   line up

    sayng perception creates reality
      as th world spirals in on itself
     never &nd always the place to be
    but are you tired of broad statements
being th only thing that really makes sense
           a n ymore

maybe it s not

incomplete moments repeatd over till they find their own endng

                    evrythng falls into place when you let it

i write to pass the time or get in touch with   the thing of it all

watching you   type   into   an orange screen
listenng to my ex boyfriends roommates music

                        entering the records

                            finding your name most places

sifting thru old friends playlsts / giggling fr no reason i can recall

los angeles

        for most of it i just thougt about yr
        s u n g la s se s   &nd how we met
        bef4or   &d
        how   they are quite handy
        f r   t i m e t r a v l ng

        i still havn t watchd   casablanca
        & i still don t really kno what t me
        it is in n ew y ork &   d
        i kno u   hav e   t he   same name
        but i m   wondrng if yur just being
        c o r d i al

th screen in front of my ey es reminds me that th strain is a choice

yu can be anywhere if you re nowhere at all

king tai

when i google th bar it is in jordan &   i ask how jordan is doing
&nd joke that people   only want to hang out to get to scoop
&nd i ve never been more   ovr th scoop   i tell you

jason says thnks a lot for putting th idea in cordelia s head but it
s not like it wasn t there befor   she s been in love with you &nd
the rest &nd i am also in love with jason   &nd the whole lot cus
were all th same obvsly but yr moving to berlin &nd i smile so big
&nd it doesn t seem like yu re so upset anymor   w th whole
someone else that
                        isn t u

                    i ll visit any time i can
                    said   last time we wer
                    here   it was warm out
                    &nd   we sat outside
                    so the   spiral begins

                    a   2 nd   v i s i t
                    fr th   m illenn ium
                    gues s i ll hav   to
                    g o   b a c k   &nd
                    change   the names or
                    s o   m e t hi   n g
                                        but

                    we ve been w r i t n g
                    a l l   a l o n g

ff

i declare i m at it again like the last time meant somethng
       a s h o r t   walk down th creek
       &nd   it   won t mattr for a bit

tryng to figure out th   difference   btwn   th subplots
       running loosly, loppng ovr one
       anothr   now & again

an affinity for   something   , or lust ,   or m v m n t
       bike lites duct-taped to th back

t o p   v i e w   o f   a   c o r n   m a   z e
       afraid of the hot cider
       at   the   polic station

linetime

dream of remembrng not t be th only 1
w/o goggles on in the   swimmng pool
to attack &nd detach w time

i hadn t dreamt of you in a while bt i held off
on th 30 minuts before bed joint   &nd
                    got m wsh

when wmn realize creativ practic fills th same needs as caretkng/
homemkng
                                s th end of th end times

th high schl cool kids shot a clip fr their clique to be th nxt in th
lineage of   th hills have eyes   bedroom movies
th buildup sequence   th culmination of feelings left
unprocessed in the field
can t stop now   is th thing   mb i should   just give in   &
                                                tune up

do yu remember rock&rollradio

how many ppl   have to say th same thing ovr bef4 it all crushes
in on itself   i feel helpless in th pursuit
an orange crush dream that i   can t stop from moving forwrd
                i wrote 1nce of envelopng th whole deal
   i surround myself wth hope   some of it seeps thru

          this is wut we re doing so i play along create a
                      way out in n eway   i can

            th sky is painted & i d like t paint 2

s

        s all th same but at differnt times
        so th culmination of all   time

makes th end result that much more   emotional

the end result being   th culmination of all time

thoughts 4 thots

whn you lookd at me and sang did yu know
evry song is alredy abt u ?

digital natives waitng for the right momnt 2 strike

every good buk needs an anthropomorphic cat

every woman i ve slept with has sprayd me w rosewater

chaotic neutral wrks out okay sumtimes

a version of each show 4r the age yu ar now -
wt wuld you like to tell me ?

i ve been seeing dead birds on the sidewalk again

yu cnnot make us all goddesses &nd expect we nt fall 4r ech othr

wen yu understand an artist s periods   lol

&nd   if so

nd if so why not keep trying he says
nd later shows me some writng

getting up to go
watchng your face

everyone is talkng about othr people not themselvs

doing it for you but you don t see me now

when spirits match up do you feel it or am i out of the water again

tell me more of the things i can and cannot do
i ll drive it off the cliff   matchbox   soap car   suitcase
home while it s raining

maybe it s the measuring that makes my heart jump aftr the fact
calm when i can nestle into thngs i already have

3am btwn

th last time i came here it was a deep shade of blu
wonderd if yu d show up   &nd sat on the couch
fr   th   first   l o n g w h i l e

                         movng between th fire &nd th floor

                                   u forget &nd forget it s
                                   been th same all along
                                   &nd i ll tell yu every time
                                   it just comes out   l i k e
                                   something about
                                   moss and rain
                                   &nd highways as usual

                                   sometimes u do things at
                                   the same time
                                   &nd sometimes my outfit s
                                   different

                               i t s   a   multi lvl game , babe

mauna

mist as cover
it s not too small

a lesson in character

some days i can t even spell

c o g n itiv   dissona nc

a   yr   since i left the city

stared at yu in th parkng lot
as you de l i ve red   msgs
f r o m t h e   p a s t

gl o w i n g   as i t r i ed to
m a i   n   t a   i   n
e   ye contact

p i e c i ng   together t h ings
i   thought i   had
b u r n t up f o r g o o d

a   gecko   climbs the pillar
of   th   house nxt   door

i   hear   y u on the phone
in th   m i d d l   of th nite
becus it is   midday
s o m e w h e r e   e l s e

testing   my   ability to do
b a s i c   m at h
on th spo t

yes &nd

at a party with x. &nd boys
walk up a long staircase
paintd portals to peer in2

x. & i fieldng qstns frm ppl
standng close to each other
i am   t o u ching   his arm
we haven t seen each other
i n   a   w h i l e

i enter into the   heat
&nd 3 women   come ovr
i hav jst movd to   chicago
i tell one of them   ::
i thnk i m gng t like it   here
as she hooks my arm   &nd
leads   me   into the party

there are 2 large areas &nd tall ceilings &nd ledges to sit on
i am in a large home &nd c. &nd
a group of ppl ar about t start an rpg
c. &nd i have plans to go to a ceremny
i ask him when he will b rdy &nd he shrugs his shouldrs
i am annoyed
i go &nd sit on th stairs
there s a group of ppl in th kitchen
d. comes over &nd starts telling me how he was lost
befor he found this group &nd
i nod becus i can relate but i don t say anythng

he leaves &nd i decide to go to a meadow
i am happy to be there by myself

cntrl arm

      they say a   mother s prayr   can bring back life
      i thnk of how t cmmunicte as i hold evrythng @ 1nce

            wht is   love but a b a t t l e cry
            what s hope but truth &nd free will
            i m reminded that i hav come here
            to f e e l what a b o dy feels like
            to feel   s t u r dy beneath my feet

                  we go to th lake
                  &nd i know yu could b any1
                    laughtr is a godsnd
                    sho me what i need

                                  i am leavng to   go home
                                  &nd e. is selling earrings
                                from a vendng machin
                                in   th e l e v a t o r
                                i end up takng more than
                                i paid fr &nd their partnr
                                says othr ppl   have been
                                doing th   same
                                i start to venmo   e. for
                                a l l o f t h e   earrings

paregoric vile or

every time i walked into work at the restaurant they were
                            playing the same song &nd
i laughd   becuse   i knw   it wouldn   t be long

pressing spaces in   the   same   way

a flowing dress   in the   meadow
of   your   parents   house

come again so i   can tell   you
th ways in which yu hav changd

sitting on the couch   while
some reality s ho w   plays in th
                            backgrnd

on my way over to yur house i stoppd at th coffee shop &d textd
you to see   if   you wantd   anythng   &nd   yu   said   no
bt you had som beer at   the house
i forgt wht th excuse was that time but it
                    seems lik a turnng pnt

only thinkng of th   windows &nd yur plasterd walls that i
understood befor i saw thm to begin wth

trinket casing

even if th tides rise &nd th sun sets quickly
        tend to th space

tend to th feelers &nd moving spines

           let th chaos complete itself
             move into th new

1-2 step

how i got here
how i flippd it all on its side & boardd a plane

      all the coffee shops in amsterdam starred in maps

            read the buks u recommended
took from them what i alwys knew i would find
& now there is something else entirely

                    it is so simple & perhaps alarming
                    the ease with which we can come
                    to believe in a whole other story

neptune

> learnd how to end it
> attemptd revision
>
> swallw me whole& up again
>
> tides against the new place
>
> chlorophyll & kerosene
>
> dancing arnd the past
> noticing what we chose to rewrite
>
> what 2c u haven't yet
> cean

> cold water down my back
> rose grape   falling   down on us
>
> submerged knots   eliminating
> th totality of someone you used 2bee
> came back down in bit form dewdrops
> slowly building back &nd braidng in
>
> clickngback in2   bones & choosing
>   a face

thchosn1

things i decide i will not tolerate nvr appear

paths out of pwr only hints & still they sting

one day ill hand it ovr
do what yu will with me

all th words already spoken

                sang songs of mars 2 u from th stage

                backlit & sprung forth
                a hologram in the mind of
                half the crowd

                let them know their truth is real
                regardless of implications

get me where

driving the element
in 8 states at once

it feels strange when i wear shoes now

i am complete
on repeat

drop the sock
realign

what do you know about

find me everywhere so i know it s real

                                                                       open th steam vent

                                                                        stone 2th othr side

                                                                        create th conditions

                                                                        exorcise each form

                    what drops
                    w/o focus

candiiland

oakland humboldt county
    sitting in the sun
   on the big island

      jade rolling & flipping coins

          writing it for the travelers bw stations

more of the same but something to remind you

      this was s. s book but i have it here now

the drums the drums

shpeshftng cellofane

fern rubbings
fern forest

remember that 1?

                        yu might not be who u think u r
                        but time for work is goo d
                        see what you want to sea
                        hear who yu wnt   again it s not like
                        u didn t know wine makes u warm

                        remembr where u woke up when

111

Ask & you shall
Pray

(doesn t matter whose)

amber brew

fwd action   falling in2 th sprng
i m   surrndd by reflctv orbs
i m   choosng 2 trus th process

not get caught up in
th amnt of time it takes 2 drill in a screw

hearing different things

havnt wrttn out the date in a while
pen running out of ink
compress the lwr back

find ur place in the cosmic unfoldng
put it to music in due time

writing like yeats thru the kamera fone

expansn from the 12 all it has evr been so
what do u want to c

othr ways to access pain & acceleration
move past it & into its counterpart

when something in u shiftd
th tides caught up to meet u where yu r

"" i wasn t on it - yu were in it ""

it fills up quickly
it   always   does
so chose carefully
what you   keep

sweep the dust
provn   undrgrnd
since   u   went

prove   nothing
realeyez it   all

sing while sleeping

                             it s a slo trip
                              a long ride

the body keep the score
  but comes back new

sent pictures to remind me of the
permanent marks on my body &
   what they meant at the time

              root to place

  anchor in that which holds tru

                             don t forget
                      when things get deep & slow
                          im a flight away
                    a 20 minute drive to eternity

save ourselvs on repeat
i love you in every form

                                        seems if you just start
                                        we ll get somewhere

twrds creation of no thing

intermittent come down
trial bw space paint

                                        give over to the next grow
                                        stretch in2 the fact
                                        give w/o expectation
                                        release consistent thread

        walk into the mmnt past where you have been
        pick up the phone & dial from somewhere else
        dream reality w/o   focus   or dimension

aho

where the sunbeams bloom   can t seem 2 finish a thought about th things i need to do around here   unrelated to th rest of it i am thermal heat & water   & th sound of something falling in th jungle   i am everyone i ve ever loved wrappd up in 1 saying look @ me now i m so fucking proud of us   i am catastrophe & the inability to look fully @ th sun when it is high above the ocean giving me food & reds   i am the lettr yu nvr wrote bubbling deep at the last post offic in the suburbs   i am a red car pummeling down the highway nearly out of gas

finishd it so now i am on2 the nxt   as th rain comes down most days & i chew on mint leaves & flwrs   it s not that it isn t enough it s just that it s a littl bit of it all that gives the full feeling   & yu
                              know i m not giving up now

i watch the coconut catapultd off the deck in yr stry where i am yu with a full beard & finger tattoos   it was what yu wantd so i went along bc   yu hav already gvn me everything

phosphorescence

triangular mvmnt   intergalactic mingle
push & pull   dispersion & chaos
repetitive mvmnts   repeatd over till they
                      find their own ending
arrangement of sequence   all is given
                             gift of grace

soulfly

old forms honor new gods
a lite by which to sea shadow pathways thru density

filament rise
monad myth

no more viewing
only site

individualize myth

small mvmnts   mediate the whole
no need 4 in btwns   or rathr b in between

gateway to   heavensent for daze

there is no need for anything but
need seeps thru & so it s
back to acid chair   acid tone

found on the road curbside   en route up the mntn

                              everything comes free

durian

things u can do

beneath the awning

      refractory period

    space bw

complete mission

                                    move sensation thru

cloroform

       th necessity necessitates
            no knowledge
           key to the edge
        belief in beginning

transparency + transference = caldera

              shoes on feet
              sedation felt
              shared &
                      unilateral

      writing at the edge of reason

what s that yu said
some closing to end it all &
come back clean

sweetness

we go home &nd in2 th dust
before time split

                                              before becoming
                                                    back again

                  green room
                  mass appeal
                creation redux

                  everything is
          bishes don t know bout an nde

skeleton dangles
catch th heartbeat

                                                      feet flat
                                                time rises
                                      completion begins

                567 what 9 wrote

                    pig trails
                    nasturtium
              delicate balance
                    spiderlily

yr past is a ghost

- edging the orbit
- off the skyline
- off the moment
- off the edge
- colloidal silver

                          list of choice
                            create the
                        master of none
                  heartbeat of the brain
                        child of mine
                           masterpiece
                             sky beam
            sky bend
            sky stage
            sky set
            sky guy
            belief

something else

telepathy is key
orbital   aeon
cat on the
week day

                                    no choice but to choose

                                    spherical nuance & delicate array

www.ingramcontent.com/pod-product-compliance
Lightning Source LLC
LaVergne TN
LVHW041306080426
835510LV00009B/878